WELCOME TO THE CONSTRUCTION SITE
Mobile Crane

Samantha Bell

Published in the United States of America
by Cherry Lake Publishing
Ann Arbor, Michigan
www.cherrylakepublishing.com

Content Adviser: Louis Teel, Professor of Heavy Equipment Operating,
Central Arizona College
Reading Adviser: Cecilia Minden, PhD, Literacy expert and children's author

Photo Credits: ©Dmitry Kalinovsky / Shutterstock, cover, 2; ©bogdanhoda /
Shutterstock, 4; ©d_odin / Shutterstock, 6; ©Anatoliy Evankov /
Shutterstock, 8; ©FotoBug11 / Shutterstock, 10; ©Viacheslav A. Zotov /
Shutterstock, 12; ©Roman023_photography / Shutterstock, 14; ©Artit
Thongchuea / Shutterstock, 16; ©A-Nurak / Shutterstock, 18; ©Anake
Seenadee / Shutterstock, 20

Library of Congress Cataloging-in-Publication Data
Names: Bell, Samantha, author.
Title: Mobile crane / by Samantha Bell.
Description: Ann Arbor : Cherry Lake Publishing, [2018] | Series: Welcome to
  the construction site | Includes bibliographical references and index. |
  Audience: Grades K to 3.
Identifiers: LCCN 2018003284| ISBN 9781534129221 (hardcover) | ISBN
  9781534132429 (pbk.) | ISBN 9781534130920 (pdf) | ISBN 9781534134126
  (hosted ebook)
Subjects: LCSH: Mobile cranes—Juvenile literature.
Classification: LCC TJ1365 .B45 2018 | DDC 621.8/73—dc23
LC record available at https://lccn.loc.gov/2018003284

Cherry Lake Publishing would like to acknowledge the work of The Partnership
for 21st Century Learning. Please visit www.p21.org for more information.

Printed in the United States of America
Corporate Graphics

Table of Contents

5   Up and Down, Side
    to Side
11 Moving Around the Site
17 Tight Spaces
19 Stable and Able

22 Find Out More
22 Glossary
23 Home and School Connection
24 Index
24 About the Author

Up and Down, Side to Side

Mobile cranes move heavy objects. They use a long **boom**.

Why would a construction site need more than one crane?

The boom can move up and down. It can move from side to side.

Pulleys and **cables** lift and lower the objects.

Moving Around the Site

Mobile cranes can move around the job **site**.

Some sit on large trucks. They can go on highways.

Some cranes can move on **gravel** roads. Some can go over bumpy ground.

Why do you think this crane has a short boom?

Tight Spaces

Small cranes can go in tight spaces. They can turn all the way around.

Stable and Able

Some cranes move on tracks. They are very **stable**. They can handle big loads.

The right crane can do the job!

Find Out More

Book

Reinke, Beth Bence. *Cranes Lift!* Minneapolis: Lerner Publications, 2018.

Website

Kiddle Kids' Encyclopedia—Crane (Machine)
https://kids.kiddle.co/Crane_(machine)
Follow the link to learn more about different kinds of cranes.

Glossary

boom (BOOM) the long arm on a crane
cables (KAY-buhlz) strong ropes made of wires that are twisted together
gravel (GRAV-uhl) small pieces of rock used on paths and roads
mobile (MOH-buhl) able to move or be moved easily
pulleys (PUL-eez) wheels with rims that have a rope or chain around them; pulleys lift heavy loads more easily
site (SITE) the place where something was, is, or will be built
stable (STAY-buhl) not likely to fall

Home and School Connection

Use this list of words from the book to help your child become a better reader. Word games and writing activities can help beginning readers reinforce literacy skills.

a	go	move	tight
all	gravel	objects	to
and	ground	on	tracks
are	handle	over	trucks
around	heavy	right	turn
big	highways	roads	up
boom	in	side	use
bumpy	it	sit	very
cables	job	site	way
can	large	some	
cranes	lift	spaces	
do	loads	stable	
down	long	the	
from	lower	they	

Index

boom, 5, 7
bumpy ground, 15

cables, 9
cranes
  how they work, 9
  what they do, 5, 11,
    17
  where they can go,
    11, 13, 15, 17, 19

gravel, 15

highways, 13

job site, 11

loads, 19

pulleys, 9

roads, 15

tight spaces, 17
tracks, 19
trucks, 13

About the Author

Samantha Bell has written and illustrated over 60 books for children. She lives in South Carolina with her family and pets.